It was there
I believed

A collection of

visual artwork and poetry

Bobbi Baugh

Writing poetry and creating visual artwork are just two different ways of thinking things through.

It makes sense to me to put them side-by-side.

©2021 Bobbi Baugh. The artwork and poetry in this book are the original work of Bobbi Baugh. No portion of this book may be reproduced or used in any way without written permission. All rights reserved.

CONTENTS

Part 1

Growing Unseen... 9

And So They Lived... 11

Blackboard Poem... 13

Floating Away... 15

Furnace Vents... 17

And All That's Gone Before... 19

History... 21

I Must Be ... 23

In Maine Driving... 25

That Grey Linen Coat... 27

It was there I believed... 29

Look Through to the Memory... 31

Mother and Child... 33

Some Strong Words... 35

This is What I want to Say... 37

A child hears... 39

In the Train Station... 41

Easter Cut and Paste... 43

Naming... 45

Why My Mother Loved Sailing... 47

Fearing the Wind... 49

Part 2

Where I am Now… 54
Cats on the Roof… 57
I like to Think… 59
Morning Sounds… 61
Pulling Weeds… 63
Naming the Robins… 64
Inner Child… 67
River… 69
Moon Poem… 71
Things That Don't Belong… 73
You Ask If I Ever Get Angry… 74
I hold this cup… 77
Fall from Grace… 79
Finding a Twenty… 81
Words for Morning … 83
My sister sends a text message… 85
Saturday… 87
To my friend who is also an artist… 89
Precious… 91
Rain… 93
Neighbors Next Door… 95
The gift of wind-less rain… 97
Turning onto Boston Avenue… 99
Consider the Lilies… 101
It seemed a good idea at the time… 102
Leaf… 105
The Air This Morning… 107

Part 1

Growing Unseen (Detail)   Textile Collage/Art Quilt

Growing Unseen

How, little girl, oh how did you

Learn this trick

Attain this superpower

Realize this necessity

Grow this shield

Of invisibility.

We Would Go to Lord and Taylor for New Spring Coats (Detail)
Textile Collage/ Art Quilt

And So They Lived

My mother had married

her silver tea service.

My father had married

his blue Mustang convertible.

From its mirrored throne on the sideboard

it commanded the household.

She polished every Saturday.

In the driveway

Nose facing the street

to be noticed by the neighbors.

He washed it on the weekends.

He said he couldn't stand

the smell of the silver polish.

She resented that way-too-flashy

bright cobalt blue.

And so they lived

Their lives.

Once She Could   (Detail)   Textile Collage/ Art Quilt

Blackboard Poem

She remembers the solid feel of her feet on the floor.

White socks in dull, closed-toe shoes that she hated.

Strapped and buckled.

She remembers the chalk in her hand, reaching for it

from a dust-filled tray at the base of the blackboard

and the way the dust would stick to her hands and fall on her skirt.

An ugly skirt with pleats.

She remembers the letters. Drawing them well.

Stick first, then add a loop.

Loop and then a stick drops down.

Now a stick and loop and a loop. Well-formed shapes.

She does not remember magic. Or words that could fly.

Another loop then a stick goes here.

She does not remember climbing fences

Or running as fast as you possibly could

With all your might. Breathing hard.

Sticks and loops and staying on the lines.

Well-formed. Well done.

Float Away in Dreams   (Detail)   Textile Collage/Art Quilt

Floating Away

It was a dream she liked, held

like a special song

to be replayed in secret.

What it would be like to float away.

On a leaf. On a stream

with meandering current. Lazy.

Drifting one hand

in the cool water, just touching

the smooth pebbles below.

But at night in her bed

she listened and

believed she heard the lapping of water

as the house itself (no! not the house) was rocked,

as the current coiled beneath it,

as the roots that held it all in place

were ripped. Their tendrils useless.

The mooring line snapped

and the house began to drift away.

Smell of turned damp earth.

And it was not like floating on a leaf.

Not like that at all.

Saying the Magic Words   (Detail)   Textile Collage/Art Quilt

Furnace Vents

She remembers the furnace vents.
Their whispering powers discovered quite by accident one day
From the basement, revealing conversation sounds
From upstairs, from the second floor.

Like holes
Cut into the house itself, into which secrets poured,
which lived and swam through the world of the vents,
moaning. The tuning sounds of an orchestra before the music.

What words were in the vents?
Could she find them, hear them,
trace their imprint in the smoky dust inside that world?

Or open up the vent
to let them spill into a towel held just right
to catch them. Bundle it so none will spill.
Run up the stairs from the basement
to the kitchen door and through
into the yellow sun by the forsythia bush
and shake them free.
Like the ghosts of dandelions, to fly away.

And All That's Gone Before   (Detail)   Textile Collage/Art Quilt

And All That's Gone Before

Only four lived in the house.

Parents and two children

In the house inside the yard

on the street with the trees

in the block with ordered homes.

Whose, then, were the other voices

And how, then, did they get into the house?

There were people in the story before the children,

People long faded away into scrapbooks

or the space below the floorboards

where memories have rooted

crawling down - down – down

through the basement into the damp earth

where, in the dark depths,

lateral roots worked at locked boxes

till their contents,

other houses – yards – streets - blocks,

were absorbed and pulled up to fill

this house – our house – with

remnants of what had gone before

Midnight Transfiguration   Textile/Paper Collage

History

I write of roots.
They probe deeply
into soil   damp. Dark earth.
Tendril-fingered
absorbing
transmuting power   energy.
Oh how I love this metaphor.

My grandmother. My mother.
The soil in which I was planted.
Sprouted.
Grew by bending towards the sun.

But I chafe against the details.
Inheritance of spirit   Character.
I cannot   know them more
now. Do not choose to.
Understand too much.

And yet. In my very bones
they comprise the marrow.
The same — as much —
as the cosmic stuff
flung out in the very beginning
to see what would stick
becoming the carbon essence
Of each of us.

It means we are all the same.
In means we are in one another.
It means they are in me.

Whether I like it or not.

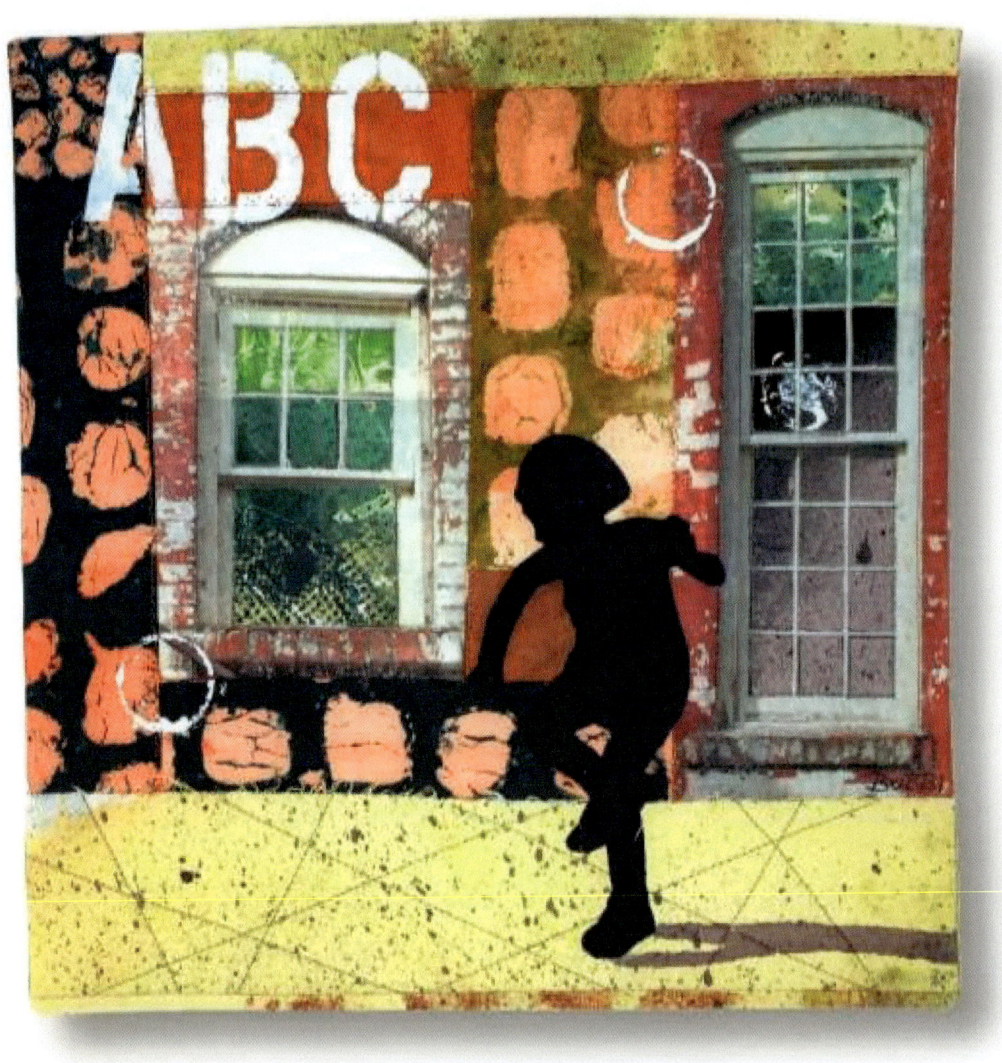

Outside / Inside   Miniature Textile Collage/ Art Quilt

I Must Be

stronger than I know.

Yoked-grey-oxen-strong

for carrying

and carrying

without falling down.

Not knowing it was heavy or that I even

carried a weight

because that is just

what walking felt like

one step

and the next

and on

and on

without falling down.

Knowing we are made of this   Textile/Paper Collage

In Maine Driving

down a curved road I looked at purple fields
my heart stopped.
My chest was weighted.

Heaviness in my lungs.
Here. It is here.
A magnetic pull
The one a great sea creature
Knows
pulling herself up on a beach.

I knew. I knew.

Every piece of the earth has its own song.
Listen for it.
Sing with it.

Every piece of the sky has its own warmth.
Bend, like a young stem growing,
to receive it.

We Would Go to Lord and Taylor for New Spring Coats (Detail)
Textile Collage/ Art Quilt

That Grey Linen Coat

Will forever be

on one of a pair of doll-like girls

holding her Easter basket

in front of new red tulips.

"click."

It was not the same as last year's coat

which was navy blue.

We had not grown that much.

The grey linen coat for spring

was about the outing

to purchase

the acting out of a good life

as it was imagined by the mother

who announced the annual trip to Lord and Taylor

the doll-like girls in the back seat

the creaking groaning house noises

ignored

as they pulled out of the driveway

and they were trying just to breathe.

Flight of the Magical Lawnchair   Textile Collage/Art Quilt

It was there I believed

I could fly

standing on the footstool

the one with cut-outs in the legs.

(I played pat-the-paw game with the dog

through the openings. It creaked.)

The needlepoint cover rough

on my tippy-toe feet.

With outstretched arms

Twinkle twinkle fingers

and seeing it so clearly

the rise and dip as I flew

above the alley and our yard.

My own brick house below.

Seeing into my bedroom window

small and dark

with one bright stripe of light

across the floor from

my friend the moon.

Look Through to the Memory   Textile Collage/Art Quilt

Look Through to the Memory

Between here (now)

And there (then)

Is not a straight path

nor an uncluttered way.

There is mist to clear away.

A fog brought forth. From inside.

My own breath on a mirror.

Condensation of memory.

A vapor of dream.

Look through. Walk through.

Walk through the cloud to see

There. Right there. I am.

I am there.

There I am.

Neither Here nor There   Textile Collage/Art Quilt

Mother and Child

The strong woman
I never knew
poured into me her strength
poured into me her secrets.
Pointed me a new way
when I was pinball directionless crashing
spinning into bells
clackers and whistles
set into motion
by a lever
casually flipped.
Her words warm oil   deep alto
resonant. Whales. Water over rocks.
All that she had absorbed and learned
given to me through sun-warmed hand
brushing my forehead.

The strong woman
I did know
zipped in her secrets
pulled the day inside herself
breathed in what had to be done
stepped into the doing of it
stood in the doorway
of each day
and willed herself to walk through.

She did all she knew to do.

Fledgling   Textile Collage/Art Quilt

Some Strong Words

For you, little girl
Because you will need them

On the day when the
cardboard box arrives at your doorstep.
Perfect. Just the right size.
The one you hoped for

And you are told to get
Inside.
It is quiet. Shaded. Safe
Inside.
Tempting as a warm bath towel.

Here, then,
Are the words
You will need:
No. No. No.
Let me out.

Here, then,
Is how you must say them:
Loud. Screaming. While running
Outside

Into the terrifying sunlight.

Small Expectations   Textile Collage on wood panel

This is What I Want to Say

that I was there.

That there was an I and it was who I am.

The replayed movies and scrapbook pictures

Were just the stage set.

There was a house

There were Easter dresses.

A dog.

And standing by the blooming forsythia

Looking at the camera

Thanksgiving. Each at our places

my father raising the carving knives

with his mile-wide "look at us!" smile

my mother raising her glass to toast

smiling in the only way she knew.

On the stage

I said my lines

made entrances and exits.

Even though I never said it

There was more.

There was an I and it is who I am.

I was there.

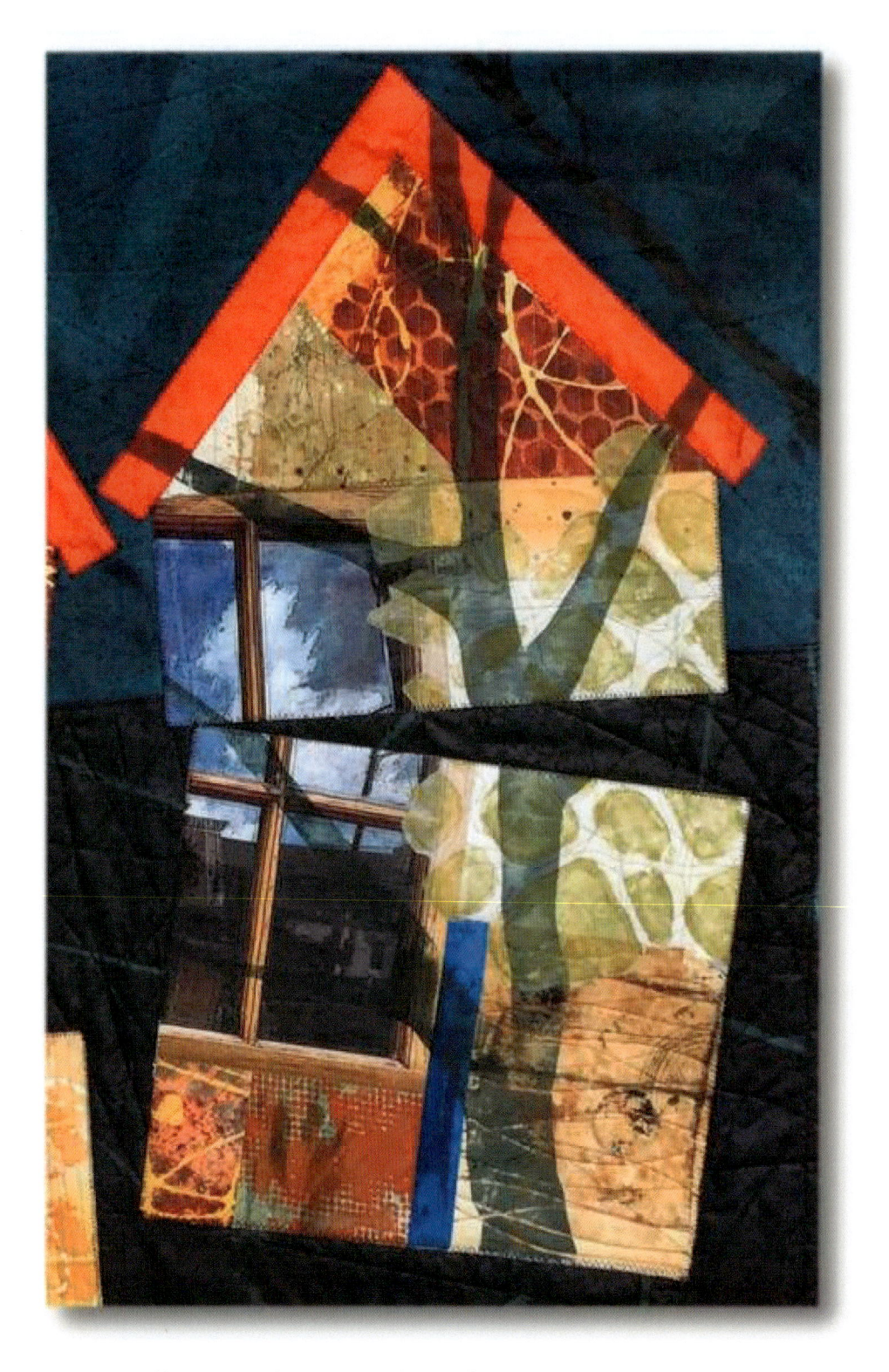

So It Will Not Break in Two **(Detail)**   Textile Collage/Art Quilt

A Child Hears

House sounds.
Keeps still. Strains
to decipher them
Their meanings. Their names.

Through the vents
through the floorboards
through the walls
up the steps. The words
muffled. Like the damper
used to make brass instruments
less harsh.

There will be a modulation.
There will be quiet.
A decision to stop
keeping still
to venture
as from slumber
to count the pieces

To arrange them into shapes.

What Were We Supposed To Be?   **(Detail)**   Textile Collage/Art Quilt

In The Train Station

My father frantic
or pretending frantic
just to work us up
to aggravate my mother
with some sense that this
is what fathers do.
We're going to miss it
We're going to miss it
We're going to miss it
As train sounds fill the void
beneath the vast polished floors
of Pennsylvania station.
We're going to miss it.

My stomach filled with fear.
Why would my mother not hurry?
We're going to miss it.
(She had other fears.
Escalators. And people
Sitting behind her in theaters.)

Held her bags
held her head high
held together by believing this
is what mothers do.

We found the platform.
The train arrived.
We departed.
We had not missed it.

Shallow Soil   Textile/Paper Collage

Easter Cut and Paste

Frozen in a scrapbook.
I am pasted in place
a child in her new spring coat.
Mary Jane shoes. White socks
and a hat — of all things!
Clutching a (new) patent leather purse.
The black and white photography disguises
the bright green behind me.
The meaning (apparently) of Easter.

Unearthed in another scrapbook.
Remnants of memory.
There she was — my mother.
A child in her new spring coat
with all the rest — the shoes
the purse — the hat!
Staring not resurrected into the camera.

With sharp scissors I snip her
from the page.
Inserted in my scrapbook, next to me,
a double.
I move her shape
place it over mine.

I disappear.

Because That's Where it all Begins (Detail)   Textile Collage/Art Quilt

Naming

The names given to us at birth
could go to anybody. Whoever showed up.
Decided before our arrival   born
of expectations. Family stories. Pouring of hope
onto the anonymous babies in a row
behind a glass window.
(Tell the truth. They all look alike)
We are first defined.

The names given to us. Later   born
of childhood taunts or
a doting grandmother
or a teacher who heard it wrong.
We are redefined.

Then shaped. And reshaped
by names applied or earned
or whispered.
Plums on the windowsill
sun-warmed and ripening
becoming our distinctly flavored selves
whose job it is
to carry what we have become.

Or create a new name.

Setting A Course   Textile Collage/Art Quilt

Why My Mother Loved Sailing

She could by God do it
If she wanted to.
The early morning walk to the water
crisp sounds of Keds on gravel
with tools — her own tools! — in her own hands.
She held them and leaned her hips and shoulders
into the task.
Scraping. Painting. Fixing
that small boat making it ready
With no voice to tell her to re-do this one, please
Or take care of a little something for me first.
The hard-chosen work was hers alone.

And when she pushed off
Into the river
And set the sail and felt it catch
the wind — the wind! — churning a rough chop
percussion on the hull that pounded her hard
but she could make that boat go.

Looking back to shore
She would see the house and the dock
The slip of sand where she had worked
growing smaller — growing smaller
As under sail she controlled
The very wind
In her own hands.

As a Wind from Another Time   Textile/Paper Collage

Fearing the Wind

Each of us is Dorothy.

Each of us lands in Oz.

From the cellar where we hide

A wind we had always feared

(Suspecting it might suck us up into a dark sky)

Does, in fact, show up to do just that.

Landing, we blink

We shake our head

Strain our eyes to focus

On this new place.

Wherever it is

Whatever it is

Here we are.

Part 2

Sometimes You Can't See In

Textile Collage/ Art Quilt

53

Where I Am Now

The house of cats is across from us.
There are a dozen. Or more.
They live to escape to our yard
To sleep under our cars.
A man lives in that house too.

The house of troubles
Is next to the house of cats.
We know little about them.
A caravan of swat-team-vested police
Showed up one day.
Nobody got shot.

The house of the good people
Is next to (on the other side)
the house of cats.
Gentle and side-by-side
This solid couple navigates life
Sets the world in order
Departs for Bible study
Every Sunday at 8:45. Exactly.

The house of Mama's voice
Is beside ours. (On our side of the street.)
That is one strong voice
It cuts through shenanigans
Of grandchildren
And across the yard to us
To call out "Good Mornin'.
How y'all doin'?"

The house of empty
Is beside us (on the other side.)
Cleaned out. Fixed up.
Readied for renters.
The beer-gut owner shows up in flip flops
Waving to us as he inspects repairs.
The last renters had chickens.

And going by now
Is the bike lady
In her always-there straw hat
And sensible culottes.
She rides early when it is cooler.
At home (the next street over)
I believe she removes her hat
And fixes a cup of tea.

From my place here
Within the screened walls
Behind the hibiscus
Hidden by palms
I breathe in the morning.
I am the observer of the houses.

I have always been a house-namer
A house-observer
An outsider who wonders at inner life.
And now I have landed
Among these houses
On this street.
Here.

Come A Tumblin' Down   Textile/Paper Collage

Cats on the Roof

On the house across the street.

It is their house.

(A man lives there to care for them.)

They walk the roof

inspecting their landholdings.

Stretch out on the sun-warm shingles

Paw through wet gutter leaves.

The black one is ready

To leap. I watch

The slow motion.

Crouch. Survey. Weigh the costs

Assess the risks

Then let go.

Falling to stretch out for the landing

On the car roof.

From my house

The house across the street

I hear a resonant thump

Of the leap. Completed.

And then the Storm was Over   Textile/Paper Collage

I Like to Think

That paintbrushes can tell.
Washed
In fresh rainwater
just collected in bowls
outside my studio window
on the work cart. Left out overnight.

The bristles natural
Responding to the memory of rain
On the animal's back
Where the oils of its body
Caused the rain to bead
Washing off running off onto the ground
Soaking
into the earth.

And that — dipped in earth hues —
my paintbrushes
are connected again
to that day that rain
that wet scent
responding to the colors
now pooling into watery shapes
on my paper.

Like old friends.

Shadow of Breath on the Air Textile/Paper Collage

Morning Sounds

There are not many.

(The point of rising early.)

From the next room

The bed creaks as

The one still sleeping turns.

From the street

The rise and fall of

Wet tires approaching. Passing.

From within the walls

An always-there hum

The sound of the house

Reassuring as rain.

And within me

Soft winds of words

Stir with the sound of pages

turning

turning.

Imprinted by the Earth   Textile/Paper Collage

Pulling Weeds

The ripping sounds of holding on.

The cry of tenacity

The hymn-prayer of "Not yet. I'm not ready."

The scent of wet earth,

microbial dwellers of a dark city.

Roots. The sound of ripping

cotton muslin into strips

so strong those fine threads

woven underground mat

designed to invade

designed to resist

designed to dig in

designed to stay put.

It will take a greater force

A sharper trowel a longer spade

To make them let go.

Letting go is hard work.

When the Song Brings you Home   Textile/Paper Collage

Naming the Robins

The movement called to my attention.
On the lawn, something happening.
Staccato motions, flurries of dark spots.
Music notes.

Leaning my chin on the sill inside the glass,
Nose just below the edge of the blinds,
A horizontal slice of life beyond.
And robins.

(Fat red robins. Infrequent.
   Wondrously arriving in unexpected flocks.)
So close… oh they were so close!
Close enough to know each one, each this-is-who-I-am,
and to name them.

Miss "I-was-here-first-in-the-birdbath" and you just
   better get on your way.
Shoo! Mine!
Miss "C'mon-it's-my-turn-now" and I'm just going to
   flutter my way right in there.
Not to be.

Did I say how close they were? So close.
Close enough to see the brightness of their eyes.
Close enough to feel, in the dark space behind my eyelids,
stroking those soft feathers.
Close enough to wonder.

Where do they hide in the hours they are not in my birdbath?
How did they choose this yard, our yard, to be their landing place today?
Today. I should mark it on my calendar.
The day I saw and named the robins,
the day my who-I-am became
crazy old namer-of-birds-woman-at-the-window.

Or the day I remembered being young and small
and entered a world of wondering and writing,
of giving voice to musings on little birds.
And stopped. Took Time. Watched. Saw.
Whichever name fits.

Did I say how close they were?

Overlooked   **(Detail)**   Textile Collage/ Art Quilt

Inner Child

I am on the porch

Watching through screen and leaves.

Listening. For birds. Morning sounds.

A ritual of newspaper and coffee.

She is here with me.

Here listening. Here being.

Here nudging to be recognized.

And remembered.

We have known other porches

Other mornings

Other hours. Quiet.

Other hours. Listening.

Song of the Rocks   Textile/Paper Collage

River

The strip of sand
not wide enough to call a beach
beside the river
takes onto itself lapping water
that moves as the tide moves
as the moon and sun
go about their celestial tasks
or as a boat creates a wake
so that standing there
with feet in the water
looking down through the green
through the light-filled darting creatures
I see my own naked feet in sand
half-covered and know
my mother   my sister
the women I see in shops
have also stood in water
looked down
felt that same water
washing over us
as we stood
and were cooled
and did not sink

And did not drown.

Keeping What Can Be Kept   Textile/Paper Collage

The Moon Poem

I could be forgiven
For believing
It was there just for me.
Perfectly centered
In my windshield

And — then a sign, surely —
That when I turned and then again
towards my destination
It was back.
Centered. Perfectly.
White. Full and wise, surely.

I was not looking for a sign.
No incantations or dances or prayers
Had put voice to any longing
Before the moon spoke to me.
It just appeared.

A gift. Given. Perfectly.
"Hello, Mr. Moon. Are you real? Are you there?"
The answer, if there were an answer,
Would be spoken to me by name. Surely.

A beloved elder, hand softly
Atop my head
And eyes and voice of years.
Of course I am real. Of course I am here
Right in front of you.

Surely, I could be forgiven
For believing.

What if One Day All the Houses Fly Away?   Textile Collage/Art Quilt

Things That Don't Belong

Are the stuff of dreams.

I am in a little boat

In a lake where (in real life)

I have never been.

There is my first grade teacher

There is our dog

A bird the wrong size

Maps of Ohio (where

I have also never been.)

I hear the sound of machinery.

Rhythmic. Pounding.

And colors form shapes

To enclose

The things that don't belong.

(The places I have not been.)

And, waking, I ask aloud

How did I get here?

Within the Harboring Silence

Textile/Paper Collage

You Ask If I Ever Get Angry

Three points that bitter biting morning.
The woman and the dog are two
On that thin strip of Maine rocks.

The woman   Distracted
on her phone or in her head
or anywhere else. But there.

The dog   Muscular black born-to-play
Adoring, longing for the game
exuberant leaps of energy beside

The woman   Going through the motion.
A half-hearted throw of the ball,
nonetheless, through the work of the plastic ball-launcher
manages a long wide arc
into

The water   The third point in the story.
Churning. Bone-chilling turbulence. Unimaginably
The dog jumps in and swims.

> *I've just never seen a dog work so hard in my life.*
> *The way she kept her eye on the ball and swam*
> *against those waves*
> *I didn't see how she could possibly make it back.*
> *It was hard hard work and she did it. She by God did it.*

The woman   Still distracted
on her phone or in her head
or anywhere else. Does not notice the triumphant return.

That. That is the point where my anger goes.
I am the superhero shooting out of the phone booth
laser beam eyes to cut through her
Freight train power to knock her down
Hell wind unfurled to push her over   take that! into the sand
Mother rage. Child rage. Unleashed.

How could you not see her?
How could you not see her?

When You Hear the Song of Memory   Textile/Paper Collage

I hold this cup

In both hands
Feel its warm contents
Through my fingers.

I want the kind of religion
that gives to this experience
a special name   a recited prayer
and a story about the ancestor
who walked in scorched fields
walked through storms of wind
carried a flaming torch
battled a wild beast
bringing home the scars
and a heart saddened for the beast.

When we drink from the cup we remember

Rich broth
Distilled   boiled down
from the bones of truth-tellers
and poured out for me
the steam inhaled burning
my throat my neck my hands
with wisdom
as drinking deep
I hold this cup
in both hands.

City Dwellers   Textile/Paper Collage

Fall from grace

The Virgin Mary has fallen
in the grass. Face down
By the driveway two doors down.

The humiliation
of weeds growing around and over
her painted concrete form.
Her underside now
exposed
the rectangular base revealing
that she wasn't — after all — real.

It is a sign.
Life has changed within the family
Gone is grand-ma-ma
to scold those crazy soccer ball boys.

Gone is anybody
who would stop to set her aright.

When Mary fell — hitting the ground
hard
she broke in two.

To Greet the Sun and Dance   Textile/Paper Collage

Finding a Twenty

In the pocket of the jeans

I wore grocery shopping last week.

Or finding in the freezer

A labeled package of homemade lasagna

I had not remembered

On a night when hunger

coincided with not wanting to cook.

The first grade class sends a Thank You

on magenta construction paper

written in their uphill misspelled words.

Turning on the radio to cello.

Yo Yo Ma and Beethoven

As I work on a Saturday morning.

A text message with a photo.

A creamy circle in a dark sky

behind still darker trees.

I am at an outdoor concert

Beneath a full moon

And thought of you.

I hope you are having a great life.

You deserve it.

Revelation   Textile/Paper Collage

Words for Morning

Be still O my soul.

O my soul. Still be.

O still be my soul.

My soul. Be.

Still be. Be.

Still.

Becoming the Song   Textile/Paper Collage

My Sister Sends a Text Message

It is morning after Thanksgiving

For breakfast she is eating pie.

I see her at her kitchen counter

Her plate. Her book. Her mug.

(She used to drink tea.

Now it is coffee.)

A simple pleasure.

Embrace it. Add whipped cream.

Forbidden foods at

Forbidden times —

Acceptance.

Veering Off Course   Textile/Paper Collage

Saturday

Across the street
Behind the house
Of the good and gentle people

Through the gate
I watch a project unfold.
Planks of wood leave the van
I hear them stacked in a pile
Hear the sing of the skill saw
See them carrying and stacking.

The workers are grandchildren
Visiting from out of state.
There are six. Teenagers.
Saturday at eight am
They are dressed. Shorts. T-shirts. Caps
Moving together in a choreography
Of helping.
Building.

I cannot see the plans
or the project
But I know what is being built
Has been built
Will stay strong
Through time.

Transcribing the Distance   Textile/Paper Collage

To my friend who is also an artist

Who would have expected
It would be now.
Now. When we've been at this
For years.
When we've spent the hours
Doing it wrong
Living our lives
Wailing at life's injuries, injustices
Dancing in the sun
(Is anybody looking?)
Or at least leaning deep into
A stone wall to absorb the heat.

All of which was required.

Between Make Believe and Memory   **(Detail)**   Textile Collage/ Art Quilt

Precious

From the driveway next door
Delightful sweetness. Pie.
To dance in.
To pour over my head like water.

The girl waiting. Grandmother takes her to school
The truck is running. Warming up.
The exhaust clouds in the morning air.

From the hood of her purple jacket little bear ears.
Backpack sparkles pink.
Thin legs — sapling limbs — in dark tights
tucked into flowered ankle boots.

I looked when I heard her soft noise.
She sang as she looked at her image
in the door of the truck.
Swaying in a dance. Singing small sounds.
Going to school. Dressed by Grandma.
Liking who she is.

Precious gem. Rare earth metal.

Beginning a New Thing **(Detail)**

Textile/Paper Collage

Rain

Falling as it does

Softly on the just and the unjust

On the roofs of those awake

And listening and those not.

On the drums of the hollow garbage bin,

My car, the cracked cement.

Something metallic next door

On the leaves opening flat their supplicant hands

Palms up — anticipating — wanting to receive.

Entering Untold Stories   **(Detail)**   Textile Collage/Art Quilt

The Neighbors Next Door

Have moved.

They are gone.

Side-by-side

At the end of their driveway

Garbage bins

Hold their belongings.

The things leftover

That nobody wants.

This morning

A crow landed

Near the bins

Then caw-caw'd

To his mates.

Together

They picked through the stuff.

Collision of Light   Textile/Paper Collage

The gift of windless rain

An invitation to enter. Absorb.

Watch its progression.

Water at first so light

Barely beyond mist. Whispering to leaves.

From the cardboard box in the bin.

The sidewalk pavers. Gentle tapping.

Then an unseen hand commands:

Ascend to power level two.

The roof at once unable to hold its volume

Overruns, water streams against porch screens

In diamonds of morning light

Sequined ribbons unfurled and flattened.

Percussion of the insistent water

Pounds out rhythm on the cardboard box.

Stay. Listen.

Through the all-the-stops-out crescendo

on box and roof and sidewalk.

And the denouement

that will follow.

The Peace of Life Chosen   Textile/Paper Collage

Turning Onto Boston Avenue

I know those shapes are people.
From context. Vertical ovals
Beside the road.
In a grey wash of fog
a quick gesture of watercolor brush.
Liquid grey.
I must depend on what I know.
Not what I see.

This is how walkers get killed.
Their matte color clothing.
Their slow movements.
Each could be a garbage can
or a bush planted just there
to barely make its shape known
to a morning driver.

She wears shorts. He wears long pants.
Two hats. Two arms connected at the elbow.
Two walking sticks for balance.
Their gait matches the sidewalk cracks
allowing time for conversation
as they walk together
In the morning emerging.

In the Familiar Fabric of Sky   Textile/Paper Collage

Consider the Lilies

In my daughter's garden
She grows day lilies.
I am seeing them in a photo.
Defying that flattened digital file
their astounding abundance
speaks to me   takes my breath.
I do not have enough crayons.
I do not have enough words
to capture what they do
to my soul.
Fullness of song   Glorious.

In our little garden I visit
the rain lilies —
the pale-skinned delicate relatives.
At the barbecue when
laughing dancing wild-haired
women in colors of the sun
take into themselves the very heat
the rain lilies — porcelain teacups
in the shade — translucent white
sit in chairs with crossed ankles
folded hands in their
lovely pink summer sheaths.

In our little garden they lift their heads
beside the plastic flamingos
also sun-bleached paler versions
of their wild dancing cousins.

Navigating the Terrain **(Detail)**   Textile/Paper Collage

It seemed a good idea at the time

Foolish lizard had the whole yard —
and I mean the whole damn yard
plus the lawn and wide world beyond
to be in!
(She could only get in the porch
through
one small opening.)

There this morning
she was. Inside the screen. Trapped.
Sometimes motionless.
A slender shape holding the mesh
by magic toes,
upside down. Waiting.

Then a snap and a darting move and
shake of the tail
as if hearing — seeing? — smelling?
a tasty snack of bug.
(Out in the wide world beyond they catch them so easily.)
Here there are not enough to sustain you.

She will soon discover
the pain of choices,
the effects of malnourishment.
All the while lacking
sufficient brain and knowledge of history
and the ways of the lawn and wide world beyond
to see the cosmic pattern of her entrapment.

I bring a glass
as if to be the savior,
catch and release and
set the world right again.
She gets away.

Now the evening is violet and cool.
I check the porch and do not find her.

This story, then, with
unseen events since first I saw her
on the screen in the sun,
has no moral pronouncement
and an unknown ending.

But that some choices
put you
in the wrong place.

Mirrored Gold   **(Detail)**   Textile/Paper Collage

Leaf

Released to find proof of land
Proof of life.
The dove returns with a leaf.

Compelled to find nesting
to layer their wren home.
Each returns with a leaf.

Bravely stomping in cool air
Child-in-the-yard adventure.
She returns with a treasure.
Pretty. Leaf.

In search of a studio subject
worthy of pencil and time
I return with a leaf.

The complex inheres in the simple.
The simple inheres in the complex.
Pretty leaf.

Becoming One With the Night   Textile Collage/Art Quilt

The air this morning

Is altogether different
from yesterday morning.
That air on my skin
Liquid-warm. Moist.
And in the grey cover
Above the house across the street
I watched planes take off
Then disappear into thickness.

The air this morning is cool
On my skin.
Wet only in that it brings to mind
Streams, fast-moving over rocks.
And the sky
Above the house across the street
Is pale blue.
I will watch planes recede
Into distant sky.

This porch. This chair. This place.
The point of the compass
Inserted firmly
So that around — all around
I draw the arc of where I am.

Bobbi Baugh creates textile-based artwork from the studio in her home in DeLand, Florida.

It is also there that she reads and writes poetry. Usually on the porch in the morning.

bobbibaughstudio.com
galleries of artwork and weekly blog

Printed in Great Britain
by Amazon